Once upon Olympus

Jenny Koralek

Illustrated by John Holder

CAMBRIDGE
UNIVERSITY PRESS

Cambridge Reading

General Editors
Richard Brown and Kate Ruttle

Consultant Editor
Jean Glasberg

PUBLISHED BY THE PRESS SYNDICATE OF THE UNIVERSITY OF CAMBRIDGE
The Pitt Building, Trumpington Street, Cambridge CB2 1RP, United Kingdom

CAMBRIDGE UNIVERSITY PRESS
The Edinburgh Building, Cambridge CB2 2RU, United Kingdom www.cup.cam.ac.uk
40 West 20th Street, New York, NY 10011-4211, USA www.cup.org
10 Stamford Road, Oakleigh, Melbourne 3166, Australia
Ruiz de Alarcón 13, 28014 Madrid, Spain

First published 1998
Reprinted 1999

Printed in the United Kingdom at the University Press, Cambridge

Typeset in Concorde

A catalogue record for this book is available from the British Library

ISBN 0 521 47630 5 paperback

Contents

Welcome to Mount Olympus

Well, you have opened my book. You have turned the page. You are now in ancient Greece, and you are standing on my mountain.

You had better come up.

No, I am not a ghost.

NO, I am not a giant.

I am a god. Yes, a god!

But come up higher, so we don't have to shout. I am tired of shouting.

Steep, isn't it? Too steep for most people. And the air is so thin, you may get out of breath. Take your time. I'm in no hurry.

There! You made it! Welcome! Welcome to Mount Olympus. Have you ever climbed so high? Or looked out across such vast distances? Or stood so far above the Earth?

Sit down! Choose a rock and make yourself comfortable.

And now I will tell you who I am . . .

I am Zeus, the great god, Zeus, the greatest of all the gods.

Zeus the all-bright, they call me.

Zeus, the bringer of light.

Yes, I am Zeus, and I rule over all other gods and goddesses.

There now, up in the sky are two of my children: Apollo wheeling the sun away till tomorrow morning, and Artemis rolling out the moon.

And the winged horse over there?

That's Pegasus.

He takes me in my chariot wherever I want to go. I'll tell you more about him and Apollo and Artemis later.

But let's get back to me: Zeus the mighty, they call me, but also Zeus the merciful, Zeus the protector of the poor . . .

And Zeus the shape-shifter.

I can turn myself into anything: an eagle, if I like – or a cloud, or a swan, or a bull.

I can turn myself into a shower of gold – or an old shoe, a donkey or a stallion, a mouse or a lion, a beggar or a king!

I am obeyed by all, feared by all, loved by all.

I know everything, I see everything, I remember everything.

When I am happy, the air is filled with the singing of birds.

When I am angry, I call up the jagged lightning flash and hurl down my thunderbolts. Then all gods, all men, all women, all children fall to their knees and cover their heads.

Even so, I, the mighty Zeus, cannot always do as

I please. There are powers older and greater than mine, powers that were here before I was born:

The sun, the moon, the stars and the rainbow,

The winds and the seas, darkness and light,

Good luck and bad luck,

Laughter and death.

All were here before me.

All come and go as they like and even I, Zeus, cannot do anything about that.

And see those three old women over there?

They are the Fates: Clotho, Lachesis and Atropos.

Clotho is spinning.

Lachesis is weaving.

Atropos is snipping.

Not for one moment do they ever cease from spinning lives, weaving lives, ending lives.

And before all these powers set to work, there was nothing here at all; nothing but Chaos, a huge empty space with a dark edge called Night and a bright edge called Day.

But let me tell you now about my family and what happened when I was born.

In the Beginning: Giants and Titans

My grandmother was great Earth herself.

First she unrolled the rivers, put the mountains in the high places, set up the forests, laid out the fields and surrounded herself in a circle of seas.

Then she married starry Sky and gave birth to twelve terrible children, the Titans. The strongest and boldest of the Titans was my father, the cruel and crafty Cronus.

Sky and Earth had other children: three Giants with many heads and arms; and their one-eyed brothers, the Cyclopes. Sky hated the clumsy Giants and the ugly Cyclopes, so he buried them deep in Earth's body, which made her cry out night and day, so great was her pain.

This made my father, Cronus, so angry with Sky that he attacked him savagely, overpowered him and chased him away for ever.

"I am ruler now," said Cronus, and he married beautiful Rhea, who was wise and good. She learned many secrets from my grandmother, Earth.

"Listen to me!" Sky thundered down to Cronus. "Listen to my terrible warning! If you do not stay on guard all the time, one of your sons will destroy you as you have destroyed me. So keep watch and be careful, very careful."

When he heard these awful words, Cronus grew so mad with fear that every time Rhea gave birth to a baby, he snatched it away from her and swallowed it down in one huge gulp.

By the time five of her babies had been torn from her arms and swallowed, Rhea's heart was like a cauldron boiling over with rage and sorrow.

So, when her sixth child was born she took a stone, wrapped it in a blanket and gave it to Cronus.

Without even looking into the blanket, Cronus swallowed the stone, thinking it was the baby.

Rhea gave her baby to Earth.

"Hide him!" she begged. "Hide him in a place where his father has no power: a place which is neither in the sky, nor on the ground!"

Earth ran to the far end of the world with that precious baby, her only grandchild at her breast. There she made a cradle and hung it on a tree-top and called up demons to guard it.

Night and day the demons circled the tree. Night and day they clattered their metal spears against their shields so that Cronus never once heard the child cry.

I, Zeus, was that child.

Shepherds looked after me. They fed me on goat's milk and honey from the wild bees and at night I slept in a cave.

I ran about barefoot on the mountain and played hide and seek in the bullrushes with Pan, my dear friend Pan, half goat, half man.

Every night I fell asleep to the sound of his flute.

When I grew up, my grandmother Earth told me the story of my birth and about my brothers and sisters lying in my father's belly. I flew into a great rage and swore to kill Cronus.

"I'll kill him!" I cried. "Just let me get my hands on Cronus and I swear I'll kill him!"

"Foolish boy!" said Earth. "That will also kill your brothers and sisters. I will help you by giving you something that will kill your father alone."

She handed me a little bottle of poison and sent me to work in my father's palace.

There I was: the barefoot shepherd boy, in a palace! The boy who once ate honeycomb in his fingers was now serving food on golden plates. The boy who drank goat's milk from a goat's horn was now pouring wine into jewelled goblets!

I worked hard and became such a good servant that Cronus chose me, his unknown son, to pour his wine at every meal.

Now was my chance to rescue my brothers and sisters!

During a banquet, while Cronus was talking to his guests, I slipped the poison into his goblet!

Cronus stirred honey into his wine, as he always did, then gulped it down.

The poison did not kill him, but it made him so sick that he threw up the stone which he had swallowed instead of me. And then – he threw up all my sisters and brothers. Suddenly they were there: my tall, proud brothers, Poseidon and Hades; my sisters, pretty little Hestia, graceful Demeter and beautiful, beautiful Hera! Unhurt and all in one piece. We hugged and kissed one another then, hand in hand, we danced for joy across the universe.

I, Zeus, led the way and I, Zeus, stopped the dance.

"We must get rid of our cruel father for ever," I said.

Then together we turned on Cronus.

In a loud voice we called for war, and the terrible small word echoed round the dark skies.

All the Titans sided with Cronus. All except Prometheus. In every battle up and down the galaxies, Prometheus fought with me. He was my great friend then, but now he is my greatest enemy. But that is another, long story, a sad one, and I will tell it to you later.

For ten years the war raged. We used trees for our bows and their branches for our arrows. Icebergs became swords and mountains became shields, but still there was no victory.

"You will never win this war," said Earth, "unless you set my other children free. Remember the Giants and the Cyclopes buried within me? Night and day they are at work hammering out weapons of terrible new power. Let them out and they will help you beat Cronus and the Titans!"

So I, Zeus, stole the keys to their prison and set them free.

The Giants exploded from the volcanoes in a rain of fire. With their hundred hands they broke pieces from the mountain tops and hurled them at the Titans, who toppled over like trees uprooted in a hurricane.

Rocks cracked open like eggshells and out clambered the Cyclopes, each swivelling his one eye to right and left, each one holding out a magic weapon.

My brother, Poseidon, chose a three-pointed spear.

My brother, Hades, chose a helmet which at once made him invisible.

And I, Zeus, chose mighty thunderbolts from which I drew jagged lightning with my fingertips.

Then we attacked our father!

As we fell upon him, the skies fell too and the whole universe went dark. The ground split open and flames shot up through the yawning gaps, setting fire to the forests. Hot winds blew blinding dust storms. Rivers flowed backwards, while colossal waves escaped from the seas and drowned the land.

Amid the dust and smoke, amid the mists and the foul fumes, Poseidon goaded Cronus with his trident; Hades, unseen, knocked his sword from his trembling hand and I, Zeus, struck him again and again with my thunderbolts.

Only then did Cronus fall, and all the Titans with him. We bound them in chains and flung them down and down into a bottomless pit where, in never-ending punishment, they are all falling still. All, that is, except Atlas. Since he had been their leader, his was the harshest punishment, and I, Zeus, chose it. I commanded him to carry the heavens on his huge shoulders for evermore.

Then I, Zeus, ordered the darkness to lift, the winds to drop, the ground to grow firm, the fires to go out.

Once more the rivers flowed towards smooth seas and a great silence fell.

As the air grew clear again, I looked down and saw these snowy peaks which almost touch the sky.

"Come with me," I said to my brothers and sisters.

And I led them across the Milky Way here to Mount Olympus and seated myself on the tallest crag.

"I am ruler now," I said. "I am the greatest god of all and you shall be gods and goddesses with me.

Poseidon, you shall rule the oceans.

And Hades, you shall rule the Underworld.

To you, Demeter, I give the care of all that grows, the corn, the fruits, the forests and the flowers.

And to you, Hestia, I give the care of all households and the fires that burn in every hearth.

But you, beautiful Hera, I want by my side. I make you Queen of Olympus itself and mother of all mothers."

Then I called Prometheus, my friend, to my side and said, "Fetch clay and mould men and women

who will worship us and look up to us for help. Make them in our image and teach them enough for simple needs. But do not let them have everlasting life like us, and do not give them the use of fire. Immortality and fire belong only to us."

So Prometheus made men and women out of clay and set them on the Earth and I, Zeus, breathed life into them. And from the very first day, as well as watching over my own family, I watched over these new mortal beings, sometimes with amusement, sometimes with anger.

Prometheus watched over them with me, but I knew he was also often watching me, as if he feared that one day his new creatures might make me so angry that I would bring down terrible sufferings on their heads . . .

Heights and Depths:
Pegasus and Bellerophon

I promised to tell you the story of my horse, the great-winged Pegasus, who came to me because of young Prince Bellerophon (who, some tell me, is one of my brother Poseidon's sons).

Poor Bellerophon! I saw it all. Looking down from Mount Olympus, I saw him kill his brother by accident in a fight and flee for protection to King Proetus in a far country. I saw the king welcome him kindly. But one day, I heard the queen tell her husband that Bellerophon had tried to kiss her, which was a great lie. It was she who had tried to steal kisses from him. I, Zeus, had seen and heard it all. But the king believed the queen and banished Bellerophon to the court of another king, Iobates, insisting that he deserved a terrible punishment.

King Iobates gave him the impossible task of killing the Chimera, a three-headed, flame-throwing monster who had been roaming the countryside, burning the land and roasting the cattle and sheep as they grazed in their fields.

But now I, Zeus, took pity on the boy. I knew, of course, that all his life Bellerophon had longed to find the strong-legged, wild-winged Pegasus. So, by means of a dream, I guided him to where Pegasus stood quietly drinking from a mountain spring.

With the magic golden bridle which Bellerophon suddenly found in his hands, it did not take him long to tame the great horse. Then he leapt onto his back and up they flew in search of the monstrous Chimera.

Suddenly, smoke billowed round them and long-tongued flames licked the sky. The Chimera was just below them, writhing and roaring and setting fire to a forest.

Pegasus snorted through his huge nostrils and Bellerophon let out a ferocious shout. The Chimera twisted her ugly heads upwards and turned her flames on them. But Pegasus was ready for her. The Chimera did not even have time to singe his tail before, with a thrust of his great wings, Pegasus flew up higher, giving Bellerophon time to draw his bow.

Bellerophon's arrows rained down upon the Chimera, riddling her from top to toe. Stabbed in her heads, stabbed in her necks, stabbed in her snaky tail, the Chimera keeled over and died and her flames died with her.

But that was not enough for Bellerophon. Oh no! His success went straight to his head.

"Now fly up higher! Higher! Higher!" he ordered Pegasus. "Take me to Olympus itself. I am ready now to live with the gods!"

Ready to live with the gods, indeed! Just because he'd killed one monster!

His pride swelled and swelled out of all proportion to this one small deed, so I, Zeus, decided he must be punished. I sent down a nasty fly which stung Pegasus in the rump. Up he reared and, bucking and kicking, flung the boy from his back. Clutching at air, Bellerophon fell to Earth with an almighty thud.

He wasn't killed, but was lamed for life and blinded by the thorns on the bush that broke his fall. As if that wasn't enough punishment, he lost all his friends too. If the gods didn't want him, they didn't want him either.

But I invited Pegasus into my stables, and whenever I feel like hurling thunderbolts, it is Pegasus who carries me in my chariot across the storm-tossed sky.

Persephone and the Pomegranate

Before I tell you about my own children, let me tell you about my sister, Demeter. As I told you, I made her the goddess of the cornfields and the harvest and when her lovely daughter, Persephone, had grown into a young woman, I commanded her to help her mother. Thanks to their tender ways with growing things, every day was a feast of flowers and fruit and fresh bread – until Hades put an end to this eternal summer, this paradise of plenty.

I had made Hades the god of the dark Underworld, where everyone goes when they die. Hades hardly ever comes up into the light from the shadowy Underworld, but one day he harnessed his black horses to his black chariot, wrapped himself in a cloak of shadows and came clattering out of the Underworld to see the sun again.

And there, in a golden cornfield, he saw Persephone picking poppies. At once he fell in love with her. He did not pause to woo her but, like a spoiled child used to getting what he wants at once, he leaned out of his chariot and snatched her up in his arms.

"Put me down!" begged Persephone. "Let me go!"

But Hades just laughed and, in a wild ride down dark chasms, took her back to his cold kingdom.

Persephone was miserable. She refused to eat anything and cried all the time.

"I want my *mother*!" she sobbed. "I want to go *home.*"

Up on Earth, Demeter was sobbing her heart out too as she walked across the world, calling Persephone, looking everywhere for her lost child.

But when she could not find Persephone anywhere, Demeter grew very angry and put a spell on the Earth. She called her spell winter. All the plants shrivelled up. The rivers turned to ice. Birds froze to death and fell from the sky like heavy snowflakes.

When I saw the eternal summer vanish, I was furious with Hades.

"Do you want us all to die of cold and hunger?" I thundered down to him. "Send Persephone back at once!"

Hades could not bear the idea of parting with his love, but I, Zeus, must always be obeyed.

"Of course you must see your mother again," said Hades kindly to Persephone. "But you must have something to eat before your long journey."

And he offered her a juicy pomegranate. Persephone's mouth watered: she was starving! So she ate six of the seeds as she stumbled and groped her way through the long passages of the Underworld, before running up into the sunlight and straight into her mother's arms.

Demeter clung to Persephone and smothered her with kisses.

"You must be hungry!" she said.

"No," said Persephone, "I just ate six pomegranate seeds."

And then Demeter let out a great cry.

"Oh, wicked Hades!" she wailed. "Oh cruel Hades! He has tricked us! For every seed of his food that you have eaten, you will have to spend a month of the year with him. Six seeds, six months! Farewell, eternal summer!"

Since that day, nothing grows for half the year. When Persephone goes back to Hades, the hot sun disappears and the corn, the fruit and the flowers vanish with her underground.

Until Persephone returns, Demeter's wintry spell covers the Earth.

One is One and All Alone:
Artemis and Actaeon

My son Apollo became the god of the sun. Daily he rides his flaming chariot across the sky. But when he has gone, it is the turn of his silvery sister, Artemis, to rule the night sky as goddess of the moon.

She is a fierce girl, my daughter Artemis.

When she was still a child I asked her what gifts she would like from me.

"I want a bow and arrow," she said, "just like Apollo's. I want all the mountains in the world to belong to me. I want some other girls to go hunting with. And promise when I grow up not to make me get married." And she danced around me, singing the old song:

> "One is one and all alone
> And ever more shall be so."

What could I do, but promise and give her everything she had asked for?

Artemis meant every word she said.

By day she liked to hunt with her friends, but at night, when Apollo had wheeled the sun away, she was busy with the moon . . .

Sometimes she hid it altogether. Sometimes she let it just peep out in a thin, silver crescent. But sometimes she ran to the top of a mountain and rolled all of it out like a huge silver ball and let it shine down on the world for hours and hours.

Artemis had a secret place where she liked to go all by herself.

It was a magic pool of the purest water, deep in the forest.

She went there to bathe and to sing her song:

"One is one and all alone
And ever more shall be so."

One day by chance, Actaeon, out hunting stags with his dogs, heard her silvery singing and, enchanted by the sound, let it guide him, step by stealthy step, until he drew close to the secret place.

He hid behind a tree and stared and stared.

He could not take his eyes off the naked beauty of Artemis.

And then, with a sharp crack, a twig snapped under his foot.

Artemis spun round and saw him at once.

"How dare you?" she said.

Her voice was cold as an icicle and perfectly calm, which frightened Actaeon more than the loudest shout.

"How dare you spy on me?" she said. "You will pay for this with your life."

And she raised a finger and pointed at him.

Actaeon felt her ice-cold anger pierce him like an arrow and charge through his blood, chilling him to the bone.

A terrible pain began to stab him in the head. He was growing antlers . . . and fur . . . and sharp hooves!

He was being pulled into a new shape . . . the shape of a STAG! The very beast he hunted with his dogs!

Actaeon tried to run, but found he was springing through the forest on four legs.

And there came his dogs, howling, baying, snarling.

His own dogs were hunting him. His own dogs who loved him and always obeyed him!

Actaeon tried to call out to them.

"Down, boys, down! Don't attack me! I am Actaeon, your master!"

But the only sounds that came from his mouth were the gasping, rasping groans of a hunted animal.

Actaeon saw the whites of the dogs' eyes. He smelled their warm breath. And then they were upon him – his own dogs.

They sank their sharp teeth into their own master's flesh and tore him to pieces.

Dimly, in his dying pain, Actaeon heard Artemis singing her song:

> "One is one and all alone
> And ever more shall be so."

Hermes the Mischief-maker and Apollo the Music-maker

Apollo is not only the god of the sun. He can tell the future. He can predict what is going to happen the day after tomorrow and the year after next.

He is also the god of mice and medicine, but above all of music. He plays the lyre so beautifully he can make the very trees dance.

Apollo was given his lyre by his brother, Hermes.

My son Hermes was born at sunrise and born naughty. He grew fast. And the faster he grew, the naughtier he grew. By mid-day he was six years old and six years-full of mischief.

"What's a big boy like me doing in this cradle?" he said, and he climbed out and ran away from home.

First he killed a tortoise. Then he scraped out the shell, tied some strings across it, plucked them, liked the sound, plucked them some more and sat there happily for a long time, making up his own music.

Then he jumped up and went down to the fields where the gods keep their cows.

He chose fifty of the best and stole them.

He covered their hooves with leaves and twigs to hide their tracks.

When he came to a quiet place, he killed two cows,

Had a good meal,

Went home,

Climbed into his cradle,

Changed himself into a baby again and pretended to be asleep.

"You naughty boy," said his mother. "What have you been up to? If it's anything to do with your big brothers or sisters you'll be in big trouble."

But Hermes said nothing. He just curled up all the tighter and made snuffling noises.

His mother was right.

The fifty cows belonged to his brother Apollo who, with the help of a witch, soon found out where they were and came to get them.

In he strode,

Marched straight to the cradle,

Shook it so hard that Hermes fell out onto the floor.

"Get up, you little rascal!" shouted Apollo. "Where are they, then? Give me back my cows at once!"

"That's no way to talk to a baby," said Hermes' mother.

"That's no baby," said Apollo. "Babies don't steal cows."

"No, they don't!" said Hermes.

And up he jumped, a little boy of six again.

Apollo seized him by the ear.

"I'm taking you to Zeus," he said. "Boy or baby, you are nothing but a THIEF and you must be punished!"

Apollo dragged Hermes by the ear all the way to Olympus. He was not pleased when I, Zeus, laughed at the story.

"Your anger," I told him, "is too great for this child's mischief."

"But this is only the beginning!" cried Apollo. "If he can steal fifty cows on his first day, I foresee that his rascally ways will grow more troublesome by the hour!"

I looked at my angry, fiery son, Apollo and then at that small boy, Hermes. I saw his bright eyes, his sharp ears, his nimble feet.

"It is true," I said. "I can't have a son of mine playing tricks all over the place. I must find him something useful to do."

"Well, Father," said the cheeky boy, "if you make me your own special messenger, I will try to behave better . . ."

I could not help smiling.

I liked the child.

"Take this golden rod," I said to him. "It shall be a sign to everyone that you work for Zeus. When you are older I will send you as a helper to the men and women on Earth. They are always getting lost on their travels. And when you are wiser you will lead them kindly, gently, down into the Underworld when they die.

Take this helmet to keep the rain off on your journeys and these winged sandals . . ."

Hermes bowed his head and solemnly took the rod, the sandals and the helmet from my hands.

"And now," I said sternly.

"Now that you are ready to work for me,

Ready to move between the worlds like a breath of wind . . .

Now . . .

WHAT DO YOU SAY TO APOLLO?"

"I'm sorry I stole your cows," said Hermes.

And he held out the tortoiseshell instrument he had been hiding in his tunic.

"This is for you, great god of music," he said.

Apollo snatched at the lyre and began to pluck the strings.

Sounds poured from his fingertips of a beauty
even I, Zeus, had never heard . . .

sweet sounds

sad sounds

sounds for every mood and every need.

Laughter was in that lyre,

laughter and lullabies.

Tears too and tunes of triumph.

And as the music poured out of Apollo into the
lyre, and flowed about us, he began to shine like the
sun itself.

He looked up at his little brother, Hermes.

"For this," he said, "I can forgive you anything."

"It is yours," said Hermes.

From that day, he and Apollo have been the best of
friends.

Hephaestus, the Blacksmith of the Gods

Hephaestus is our blacksmith.

In his forge beneath the volcano, Mount Etna, helped by his golden robots, he makes perfect weapons and fine jewellery for all of us.

His skill is of the finest, yet he was born with an ugly face and a lame foot.

"I don't want him! He's hideous!" shrieked his mother, Hera, whose beauty makes her vain. "He's no son of mine!"

And she picked him up and threw him off Mount Olympus.

For one whole day, Hephaestus fell through the air. He landed in the ocean and was rescued by the gentle goddess, Thetis, who loved him and looked after him in her cave beneath the sea. It was here that he set up his first smithy, where he made bowls and dishes for Thetis as well as pretty trinkets.

When he grew up, Hephaestus decided to pay his mother back for being so cruel to him.

He made her a most beautiful pair of glittering sandals and sent his golden robots up to Olympus to lay them at her feet.

Hera was flattered.

"Exquisite!" she said. "Nothing but the best for me, of course. After all, I am his mother."

She thrust her feet into the sandals and admired herself in them. But when she tried to stand up, she lost her balance. With her bottom in the air, down she fell, flat on her face.

Underneath their glitter, those sandals were made of lead.

I, Zeus, laughed and all the gods and goddesses laughed with me. Our unkind laughter bounced off the rocks like hailstones off a frozen lake.

Hera was ashamed: she knew why Hephaestus had played this trick on her.

But when the golden robots told Hephaestus what had happened, he felt sorry for Hera. For all his gruffness, he has a kind heart. He came straight up to Olympus from his forge with a pair of sandals made of real gold. He lifted Hera up and took the heavy sandals off her feet and knelt to put the new ones on.

"I'm sorry, Mother," he said.

"And I am sorry too," said Hera.

Then they kissed each other and forgave each other and I, Zeus, rejoiced, and all the other gods and goddesses with me.

Hera built Hephaestus a new forge here on the mountain, and whenever he makes necklaces, Hephaestus always gives her the best one.

The Labours of Herakles, the First Hero

Hera, my wife, hated my dear son Herakles, the mighty hero.

Her heart told her that he was very special to me. But she was jealous, because he was not her son.

For I, Zeus, had many times gone down to Earth in disguise and married nymphs and ordinary women, who had given birth to extra-ordinary children, half-human, half-divine.

Hera had sent snakes to kill Herakles when he was still just a baby. But when her huge pythons slithered into his cradle, he strangled them in his chubby hands with his already powerful wrists. Her failure to destroy him enraged Hera, but she bit her lips and waited until Herakles grew up. Then she put such a strong spell of madness on him that he killed Megara, his own beloved wife.

When the madness wore off and he saw what he had done, Herakles almost died of sorrow.

He left his city and went to Delphi, to my temple. There he fell on his knees and begged me to help him.

"Can I ever be forgiven," he asked me, "for killing my own wife?"

"No," I said. "Not unless you are willing to labour

for many years at twelve almost impossible tasks that will challenge your courage and cunning to the very limit and beyond."

"But surely you will help me?" he asked.

"No, my dear son, I cannot," I answered sadly. "I have made a sacred promise to Hera that you and you alone will undertake these labours."

"Very well," said Herakles calmly, "but tell me, at least, where to begin."

"You must go to King Eurystheus," I said. "But I warn you, he is in Hera's pay and will do his utmost to kill you."

The king sent Herakles off at once to kill a monstrous lion who lived in a cave. Many men had tried to kill it, but the lion always managed somehow to escape.

Herakles did not immediately rush into the cave as others had foolishly done. Instead he crept silently round to the back of it, where he found a large hole, hidden by brambles and bushes.

He quietly blocked up this second, secret way out and then rushed into the cave, charged at the lion and strangled it, just as he had strangled the snakes in his cradle.

Herakles then slung the lion over his shoulder and took it back to the king.

The king had never imagined he would ever see Herakles again.

When he saw him coming with the dead monster on his back, he was so terrified he jumped into a big stone pot.

"Get back!" he squealed. "Get back! Don't come any nearer. I can see the lion is dead. Aren't you brave? Just stay where you are, and I will shout to you what your next deed is."

Every time Herakles came back from another dangerous adventure, the cowardly king almost died of fright.

Every time he hid in the big stone pot.

Every time Herakles had to leave the ever growing pile of monsters and magic creatures he had killed outside the walls of the king's city.

It was Herakles, this great hero and dear son of mine, who gave Atlas the only rest he has ever had from carrying the weight of the heavens on his shoulders.

The cowardly king had sent Herakles to fetch some apples from a tree in an orchard in a land beyond all seas.

But this was no easy task: Earth had given the tree to Hera as a wedding present and the apples which grew on it were golden. The tree was guarded day and night by the Hesperides. Lovely nymphs, the Hesperides, but fierce as tigers.

Herakles walked the land and sailed the seas for a year and a day, but he could not find this land at the far ends of the world. The nearer he seemed to get to it, the further it seemed to move away. At last he could bear it no longer.

He fell to his knees and called up to me.

"Zeus! Zeus! Help me! I am so tired and I cannot find my way."

But I did not answer Herakles.

My heart ached for him, but I could not break my promise to Hera that I would not help him with his difficult labours.

No. I did not answer Herakles when he called to me.

He looked up one more time in despair and then . . .

He saw Atlas almost breaking his back under the weight of his eternal load.

"He must be able to see for miles and miles," said Herakles. "Since no-one else will help me, I must help myself with all my wits and all my cunning."

He went closer to Atlas and called up to him.

"Good day, great Titan! You must be very tired."

"I am indeed," sighed Atlas.

"It was a cruel task that Zeus gave you," said Herakles.

"It certainly was," said Atlas.

"From where you are standing," said Herakles, "can you by any chance see the land where the Hesperides live?"

"Of course!" said Atlas. "I can see everything, everywhere, every day, all day and all night."

"How lucky you are!" sighed Herakles.

"Lucky?" groaned Atlas. "Lucky? If you had been here as long as I have, you would be bored to death by the view."

"Well, then," said Herakles swiftly. "Give the load to me and have a rest. Better still, give your load to me and go for a long walk. And perhaps while you are stretching your long legs, you could stride over to the land of the Hesperides and bring me some apples from that tree?"

"Is that all?" said Atlas with joy. "Why, for the

man who takes this burden off my back I will do anything!"

So Herakles took the heavens off the Titan's back and Atlas went to fetch the apples.

Atlas was not a fool. He saw he now had a chance to escape.

"I've got the apples!" he called up to Herakles. "I'll just go and take them to the king . . ."

But Herakles was no fool either.

"Very well," he said. "But could you just take this load off me for a minute? It is so heavy it is hurting my head, and I need to find something soft to rest it on."

"All right," said Atlas.

And before he knew what he was doing, he was trapped again.

"I am sorry," said Herakles, "and I thank you for your help. But I have my own work to do, as you have yours."

He hurried back to the cowardly king hiding in the big stone pot.

"Get back! Get back!" the king shouted. "I don't want the apples. Keep them!"

But Herakles did not keep them.

He gave them to the goddess Athene, and she gave them back to the Hesperides, those fierce nymphs who guard them still in that land of mystery at the ends of the Earth.

It would take a thousand and one nights to tell you all there is to tell about the adventures of Herakles.

How he slew the Hydra, who grew two new heads for every one of the hundred he lopped off and whose every vein was filled with poison instead of blood.

How he cleaned out in a single day a century of stinking cattle-dung from the stables of King Augeias. How he scared off the brass-beaked killer birds of Styphalus by banging on the mountain tops with giant castanets. How he killed the Queen of the Amazons for her golden girdle, yet hunted the golden hind of Artemis for a year and a day before catching it without touching a hair of its head.

And who but Herakles had the courage to go down into the Underworld to fetch up the fierce-fanged guard dog, Cerberus, beloved of Hades? Who indeed but Herakles, his hands flying fearlessly straight to the hell-hound's throat, half choking it to death, only to be told, when he tried to present the beast to King Eurystheus, to take it straight back again.

The labours of Herakles were indeed almost impossible. But he never gave up. With courage and cunning, he completed them all. And when at last he died, he did not go down to the dark Underworld as ordinary mortals do.

I, Zeus, went down to Earth and brought him up to Olympus. I made him a god and gave him my gentle daughter Hebe as his new bride.

51

The Judgement of Paris

My loveliest daughter is Aphrodite. Fresh and rosy as the dawn, soft as summer twilight, she was born to the sea-goddess, Dione.

Lithe as the lynx, dangerous as the viper, with violets in her eyes, lashes like butterfly wings and lips like red cherries, she rose up one day out of the white sea-foam, riding in a shell.

Her laughter streamed towards me like water rippling over rounded pebbles, and the scent of orange blossom floated on the air.

What could I do but make her, there and then, the goddess of love?

With her beauty and the magic girdle at her waist, Aphrodite can make anyone fall in love with her, both gods and men. But this does not always make them happy.

I, Zeus, was once at a wedding on Olympus. All the other gods and goddesses had been invited, all except old Strife with her warty chin and her crabby tongue. Strife loves a quarrel, and who wants to quarrel at a wedding?

Just as my daughter Hebe was filling up our goblets with wine, old Strife rushed in and threw a golden apple on the floor.

"Here's a game!" she screeched. "A good game! Who's the loveliest, eh? Who's the fairest, eh? Go on, then! Choose! Choose! The apple goes to the fairest of all!"

I, Zeus, rose up and ordered her to leave, but her ghastly cackles left nasty echoes in the wedding hall.

Aphrodite, with her sister Athene, ran with Hera, my wife, to grab the apple and began to squabble over it.

"You've only to look at my lovely, serious, grey eyes," said Athene, "to see that I am the fairest . . ."

"Oh no," hissed Hera. "Look at my lovely, soft arms. I've always been the fairest by far . . ."

Aphrodite laughed at them.

"Give me the apple," she said, stepping between Hera and Athene. "It is not enough to have lovely arms or lovely eyes. The apple is meant for me, because since the day I rose out of the sea I have been entirely lovely from the crowning glory of my hair right down to my pretty feet."

And because they knew this was true, Hera and Athene began to fight with Aphrodite over the apple until I ordered them to stop.

"I want nothing to do with this nonsense!" I

thundered. "Let the handsomest man on Earth settle this silliness."

"That will be Paris, of course," said Aphrodite.

"Of course," said Athene.

"Who else?" said Hera.

And they went dashing down to Earth with the apple to find him.

Paris was astonished when three goddesses landed in the field where he was guarding his sheep.

They went up to him with their sweetest smiles.

"You must choose," Aphrodite murmured. "You must choose who is the fairest of us all!"

Hera held out her graceful arms to Paris and said, "If you give *me* the apple, I will make you the greatest of all kings."

Athene gazed at him with her large grey eyes and said, "If you give *me* the apple, I promise you will win every battle in every war."

But Aphrodite stood on tiptoe and draped her magic girdle round Paris's neck and stroked him gently on the cheek.

"Give *me* the apple," she said, "and I will give you the love of the loveliest woman on Earth."

Of course Paris gave the apple to Aphrodite, who kept her promise, which led to nothing but sorrow, because the loveliest woman on Earth was Helen, who was already married to Menelaus, the king of Greece.

But Paris did not care. He stole her away anyway. Stole her away to Troy, his father's kingdom. All the warriors of Greece came after him in their great ships, and for nine long years a great battle raged to keep Helen there.

Yet in the end, Aphrodite's promise was the death of Paris and of many other even greater heroes.

Perseus and the Gorgon's Head

I, Zeus, was astonished that my favourite daughter, Athene, took part in that foolish beauty contest.

She is, after all, the goddess of wisdom.

Athene was born from my head.

Out she leapt, wearing a helmet, carrying a shield and a spear, with an owl perched on her shoulder.

She at once set about showing the mortals how to do things: she taught the men how to make ships and chariots, ploughs for the fields and bridles for their horses. She showed the women how to spin and weave. Athene is vain about her spinning. Only the other day she turned a poor girl called Arachne into a spider, because Arachne's work was even better than her own.

She likes a fight – as long as it is fair – so of course she was ready to help the daring Prince Perseus to kill Medusa, the Gorgon.

Perseus was born to me by the mortal queen Danae, after I had visited her one night in the form of a great shower of gold. Her husband cast her and the baby out to sea in a wooden ark. It was washed up on the shores of the kingdom of Polydectes, where a kind fisherman rescued them and sheltered them.

Years later, King Polydectes caught sight of the lovely Danae, fell madly in love with her and tried to marry her against her will. Perseus refused to let the king have his way and fiercely defended his mother. Polydectes never forgave Perseus and hate was still in his heart when later he married another princess.

When he demanded lavish wedding gifts from all around him, my foolish son offered to bring him anything he asked for.

"Very well," said King Polydectes, rejoicing at the chance to be rid of Perseus for ever. "Very well. Fetch me the Gorgon's head!"

Fetch the Gorgon's head!

The Gorgon's hissing head!

Her hair was a mass of writhing, poisonous snakes!

Even I, Zeus, was aghast.

No man who had gone to hunt the Gorgon had ever come home again.

No man on foot had a chance to escape the lightning moves of the swift-winged Gorgon.

But worse, far worse: one glimpse of her hideous face with its long, lolling tongue turned any man to stone.

I, Zeus, shuddered for Perseus. What would that great prince do?

He went straight to Athene and fell at her feet.

"I can't do it!" he cried.

"Yes you can," said Athene firmly, "with the help of a helmet to make you invisible, a bag to put her head in and a pair of winged sandals to fly away on."

"But where will I find all these things?" groaned Perseus.

"They are guarded by nymphs," said Athene, "but even I do not know where they dwell. You must ask the Gorgon's ancient, long-necked sisters to show you the way. They have only one eye and one tooth between the pair of them. You must first steal the eye. Steal the eye and they will be blind. Say to them you will not give it back unless they show you where to find the nymphs.

And now, Perseus, remember this! When at last you enter the Gorgon's lair, you must not look at her. Not once. Seek her out in the shining mirror of your shining shield."

Perseus found the Gorgon's sisters in a cave.

He had never seen such a hideous pair of old hags.

And there was the eye, on the filthy floor.

"Give it to me!" the first hag was shrieking. "It's my turn!"

"I haven't got it!" the other hag was screaming.

"You must have dropped it! I haven't got it!"

"No," said Perseus. "I've got it."

And the old hags set up a caterwauling worse than fifty lovesick cats.

"Who's that?" they screeched.

"What do you want?" they yelled.

"Give us back our eye and we'll do anything for you! Anything!"

Perseus pushed them apart, grabbed the eye and held it high above his head.

"First tell me where to find the nymphs who guard the magic helmet, the sandals and the bag that I have been sent to fetch by the goddess Athene!"

The Gorgon's sisters trembled at that name. Desperate to get back their one and only eye, they quickly told Perseus all he needed to know.

As he left the cave, he tossed the eye onto the cave's dirty floor, where the hags are scrabbling for it still.

The nymphs willingly gave him the magic weapons, and with the winged sandals on his feet, the bag slung over his shoulder and invisible in the helmet, Perseus was soon creeping into the Gorgon's lair.

She heard him. She heard him, but she could not see him.

In vain she thrashed about as he came closer, ever closer.

Perseus trembled at the hiss of her snaky hair. Her hot stinking breath burned his cheek. He was close enough now to see the Gorgon's face.

But Athene's words came back to him: "You must not look at her. Not once. Seek her out in the shining mirror of your shining shield."

At once he thrust his shield in front of him and caught the Gorgon's reflection in it. Perseus seemed to feel Athene's hand on his sword arm, which gave him the courage to keep looking steadily at that dreadful writhing head in the mirror of his shield. With one blow, he chopped off the Gorgon's head.

He dropped it into the bag and flew away.

Perseus went straight back to King Polydectes and, thrusting the Gorgon's head in his face, said calmly and coldly, "Here is the wedding gift you wished to receive from me."

Before the king could speak or flee, he was turned to stone. He stands there still, a silent statue.

Then Perseus, still carrying the dreadful head, turned on his heel and went to find Athene. When he had found her, he knelt at her feet and said, "Only you, great goddess, deserve the power which lies in this head."

And Athene smiled on Perseus, and took that snaky head from him and placed it in the centre of her shield, to petrify anyone foolish enough to make of her an enemy.

Dionysus and the Pirates

The god Dionysus is the wildest of my children.

He lives in the wild mountains with his wild friends: noisy nymphs and strange satyrs, half-man, half-beast. It was Dionysus who discovered how to make wine from the grapes that grow on the hot hillsides. He loves to rampage down the mountain and into the silver-green olive groves with his friends, singing, dancing and drinking wine.

But Dionysus was not like this as a child.

When I see him now, carousing with his companions, all filled with a mysterious, frenzied energy, I often ask myself what happened to the lonely boy I used to watch as he roamed in solitary places on his own. For this wild son of mine, who was not a child of Hera's, had had to keep out of her jealous way since the day he was born.

One day he found an empty island and played there alone.

He played shipwrecks. He played pirates. And when he was tired, he lay down in the sand in the shade of a tree and fell asleep.

Rough voices woke him up.

A circle of real pirates – filthy thugs and cut-throats – stood round him.

"Well, well, well!" said one. "We came ashore for fresh water and a few dates, but what have we here?"

"A young prince, by the look of his fine clothes," said another.

"Take him on board!" their captain commanded. "Some king will pay us a great sum of money to get this beautiful buccaneer back!"

And they dragged him to their ship where they stood round him, jeering and tugging at his thick, long hair and pulling at his fine clothes.

All except the helmsman. He was not a pirate, but a poor man who had taken the job of steering the evil ship because he needed the money.

Somehow he found the courage to speak up.

"Leave the boy alone!" he begged. "How do you know he is a prince? His beauty is so strange, so fierce, perhaps he is a god."

"Keep your mouth shut!" sneered the pirates. "Or we'll heave you overboard."

And they fetched a rope and tied Dionysus to the mast.

At once the sky went dark and although the sails were filled with wind, the ship stood still and a flute began to play.

The ropes round Dionysus fell off by themselves.

The sea turned to wine the colour of blood.

And vine leaves twined themselves round the ship's mast.

The pirates' oars began to bend and bow like thin trees in a tempest and then . . . the oars turned into writhing snakes.

The pirates were terrified.

They dropped their oars and huddled together.

Snarling panthers, roaring lions and growling grizzly bears came lunging up the gangways. The pirates turned tail and leapt, one by one, over the side of the ship.

As they did so, one by one, they all turned into

DOLPHINS.

Only the helmsman was left, petrified, at the wheel of the ship. He was dumbstruck, but full of pity for the pirates. And then, through his fear, he heard the voice of the great god speaking to him.

"Because you have a good heart," said Dionysus, "because you tried to save me and because these dolphins were once men, I make a solemn promise . . . Dolphins will always be friends to mortals."

And he placed one dolphin in the sky. At once it turned into a star, there to remind anyone who looks up at night that they have friends in the seas who were once as human as they are.

I, Zeus, hope that this reminder will work. I hope that all men, all women and all children will always be friends to dolphins.

King Midas

Dionysus himself told me the story of this foolish king. He found it amusing, but it made me both sorrowful and angry. I began to wonder if I had been wise after all, when that day long ago I had allowed Prometheus to make these mortal creatures.

Dionysus has one great friend among the noisy crowd that rampages down the mountain and through the olive groves, singing, dancing and drinking wine.

His name is Silenus, the oldest and the wisest of the satyrs.

One hot day, Silenus drank too much wine. It made him very sleepy, so he wandered off by himself to find a good place to have a nap.

He came to a beautiful garden, lay down in a flower-bed and fell asleep.

The garden belonged to King Midas.

King Midas was a foolish king who wanted more than anything else to be the richest man in the whole world.

He had a lovely daughter, a fine palace, a garden full of roses.

He had clowns to make him laugh, clowns to make him cry.

He had musicians to sing for him at supper, and story-tellers to tell him tales at bed-time.

But he had no gold.

By day his fingers itched and twitched with his longing for gold, gold, gold.

At night he dreamed of nothing but . . . gold. Gold coins he could count in tens, in hundreds, in thousands, in millions.

Heaps of gold . . . mounds of gold . . . mountains of gold . . .

He dreamed of a crown for himself made of gold . . . a palace of gold . . . and every single thing in it made of gold.

He dreamed of rings galore for his daughter, and bracelets and necklaces and ear-rings all made of gold.

He even dreamed his roses were made of gold.

"If only," he sighed, "if only everything I touched turned into gold then I would be the richest man in the whole world."

One hot day he was sitting in his palace

dreaming as usual of gold, when his gardeners came in with sleepy old Silenus.

King Midas welcomed him, of course, because even he knew that Silenus was the best friend of the great wild god, Dionysus.

He made a feast for the old man, and then Midas himself took him home through the dark woods and up the mountain paths back to Dionysus.

"You must be rewarded for looking after my old friend," said the great god to Midas. "Perhaps you have a wish which I could make come true for you?"

"Oh yes!" said King Midas, his fingers itching more than ever. "I have always wished more than anything that whatever I touched would turn to gold!"

"Are you sure you want this wish to come true?" asked Dionysus.

"Oh yes!" said King Midas. "I am sure. Quite, quite sure."

"Very well," sighed the great god. "It shall be so."

King Midas could not wait to see if he really could turn things to gold.

First he touched a leaf on an oak tree.

It turned to gold.

Then he picked up a pebble and . . . it turned to gold.

Next he scooped up a lump of earth. It turned into a nugget of gold.

By now he was so excited that he rushed into a field and flung his arms round a sheaf of corn.

It turned at once to gold.

"It works!" shouted King Midas. "It really works! Everything I touch does turn into gold! I'm rich! I'm rich! And that's just the beginning! Before I go to bed tonight I will certainly be the richest man in the whole world!"

By the time he got home, King Midas was hungry and thirsty.

The servants spread the table high with bread and meat.

He seized some bread. But long before it reached his mouth, it had turned as hard as stone: a golden stone.

King Midas tried the cheese and the grapes, the oranges, the plums and the pomegranates. But they all turned to gold. He could not get his teeth into anything.

He poured himself some wine, but as soon as it touched his lips it turned into liquid gold.

By now King Midas was very frightened. He was famished. His throat was as dry as a leaf in winter.

"What have I done?" he said. "If I cannot eat or drink, I will die."

He began to tremble and sweat, so he tried to take his cloak off. It turned to gold, heavy as lead.

And then something very terrible happened.

His daughter came into the room. When she saw her father she came running to kiss him. King Midas stepped back and flung up his arms. "Don't!" he cried. "Don't touch me!"

But it was too late.

His daughter had touched his fingers and turned to gold.

King Midas took one look at his child standing there, a golden statue, and then he began to run. Out of the room, out of the palace, through the garden, into the woods, up the mountain paths, all the way back to Dionysus.

"I made a mistake," he sobbed. "A terrible mistake. Oh great god, please, please take away my golden touch!"

"I cannot take back my gift to you," said Dionysus.

"B– but what shall I do?" wailed King Midas.

"You must find the place where the river begins, where the water is purest and there you must wash yourself from head to toe. Only then will you lose your golden touch. Everything will be as it was before. But remember: once again you will have no gold."

"I don't care!" said King Midas. "I don't care."

And he ran and ran, all the way to the place

where the river begins, and washed himself in it from head to toe.

Then King Midas hurried home, his cloak light again and blowing in the breeze.

And there, running to meet him, rosy and laughing, was his daughter.

King Midas hugged her and kissed her and swept her up on to his shoulders.

Together they sat down to eat and drink.

Never had bread tasted so fresh and cheese so salty and fruit so sweet and wine so sharp.

And the gold?

It had all trickled into the sand on the river-bed where it can be seen to this very day.

Punishment for Prometheus

As time went by, I, Zeus, began to grow more and more impatient with the mortal creatures on Earth. I thought of Actaeon and Bellerophon, of Paris and Midas, of cruel pirates and cowardly kings. My son Hermes, who never ceases to move between the two worlds on his winged sandals, invisible to all in his winged helmet, was always bringing me fresh stories of mankind's antics.

"How foolish humans are," I sighed one day, as Hermes and I watched the miserable creatures. "How greedy and inquisitive, how boastful and vain."

"They can be brave, too," said Hermes.

"But never without our help," I replied. "And they are always so ungrateful. But what can we expect? They look up and see us behaving like them. It cannot go on like this."

Then I sent Hermes down to Earth with my command that if men and women wished to keep my goodwill, from now on everyone must give me their best sheepskins, their best goatskins, as well as a part of every meal, a sip from every flask of wine and a sheaf of corn from every harvest.

"And you may tell them," I added, "that if they

are not prepared to make these sacrifices to me, I will destroy them utterly."

Then I called a meeting of my own family and ordered them to behave as it befits gods and goddesses to behave and to stay up on Mount Olympus and have nothing more to do with the men and women of Earth.

How they all trembled at my words!

They were all far too afraid of me to disobey.

But just for good measure, I then rode out across the Universe, rolling my thunderbolts before me, and everyone on Mount Olympus and on Earth hid from me.

Everyone, that is, except Prometheus, that great Titan who had fought at my side in the war against my father. Prometheus, who had been my friend, now became my enemy.

Prometheus now betrayed me.

Prometheus now tricked me.

Later I remembered that day long, long ago, when he and I, side by side, had watched these mortals, made by him out of clay and brought to life by my breath. I remembered how Prometheus used to look at me anxiously from time to time, as if he knew I might lose patience with these toys of mine one day. Perhaps he had been waiting a long time, in fear and dread, for this day.

It seems he felt sorry for the mortals as he looked

down on them looking up at us, shaking with fear at my words, lost and helpless without the presence of my sons and daughters in their world.

It seems that he had always felt sorry for them, because I had refused to let him give them FIRE, which means they eat their meat raw and bloody, and shiver at night when the sun goes down.

It seems that he decided to help them, whether I wished it or not. Prometheus picked up a long stick and crept up to Mount Olympus. My own daughter Athene, my favourite child, let him in through the back door.

He crept into the stables and thrust the stick into the flaming wheels of Apollo's sun-chariot. When the stick began to glow like charcoal, he broke a piece off and hid it in a fennel-stalk and took it down to Earth.

"I have brought you fire from the gods themselves," said Prometheus to all the men and women. "Now you can roast your meat and keep yourselves warm at night."

When I found out what Prometheus had done, I terrified all creatures with my anger, from my wife to the lowliest worm.

My lightning flashed across the sky and out of my thunder I called down to everyone on Earth.

"Fools and idiots!" I roared. "You will pay for this and so will your children and your children's children. And as for your friend, Prometheus, he will pay for this for all eternity."

And I ordered Hephaestus, blacksmith of the gods, to make chains for Prometheus and bind him to the side of a huge rock among the high mountains of the distant Caucasus.

Then I sent an eagle to peck out his liver.

Every day the eagle pecks out his liver and every night it grows again.

Such was my anger.

Pandora and the Box

But my anger did not stop there.

Once more, I called Hephaestus to my side. "I am not ready to let you go yet," I said, "because there is one more thing I want you to do to punish those idiots who live down there on Earth. I want you to make a woman who is beautiful to look at, but clothed in silliness and stupidity, spitefulness and lies."

Hephaestus did as he was told, but I know it was with a heavy heart.

When he had made the beautiful woman and clothed her, he brought her to me and I, Zeus, breathed life into her.

"I name you Pandora," I said. "Pandora, which means 'all gifts' – and what gifts they are!"

Then I laughed. Yes, I laughed cruelly.

"And here, my dear Pandora, is your husband, Epimetheus."

I saw all the gods and goddesses look at each other, wondering what I was going to do to Epimetheus. He is the brother of Prometheus and as dim-witted as his brother is clever.

"Go now!" I said to the husband and wife. "Go now, the two of you, and make your life on Earth."

As soon as Pandora and Epimetheus had left,

I sent for Hermes, my winged messenger.

I handed him a box, richly carved and studded with jewels.

"Take this down to the happy pair," I said. "Tell them it is my wedding present to them."

When Epimetheus saw the box, he was afraid.

"I don't think we should open it," he said to Pandora.

"Not open it?" shrieked Pandora. "Not open a present from Zeus himself? Why ever not?"

"Prometheus told me never to take any gifts from the gods," said Epimetheus, looking sadly at his beautiful, stupid wife.

"Well, more fool him!" sneered Pandora.

And, before Epimetheus could stop her, she opened the box.

Like a swarm of angry bees, out flew all the nasty things that are still in the world today. Out flew aches and pains and itches and scratches and cuts and bruises and coughs and colds and hiccups and hayfever. Out flew stealing and lying and pinching and kicking and bullying and meanness, bad dreams and all the terrors of the dark.

They fell upon Pandora like a black, buzzing crowd and beat her black and blue before they flew away screeching to make life a misery for everyone else on Earth.

Pandora was screaming and sobbing.

"Shut the box!" she kept yelling. "Oh Epimetheus! What are you waiting for? SHUT THE BOX!"

Epimetheus was about to bring the lid down with a bang, when he heard a voice calling from the bottom of the box.

It was a sweet voice, calm and clear.

"Let me out!" it said. "If you are wise, you will let me out."

So Epimetheus cautiously lifted the lid and out flew . . . HOPE.

"Hope?" I said to Hermes, when he had finished telling me this tale. "How did Hope get in there?"

But Hermes just smiled.

"Look down," he said, "and you will see her at the Rainbow's end, laughing . . ."

"What a piece of luck for mortals," I sighed, "that she found her way into that box."

And I remembered those powers greater than mine: Laughter, Luck, and the Rainbow, and bowed my head before them all.

Hope did not leave Epimetheus and Pandora,

but stayed with them through the bad days and the good days.

Pandora gave birth to a daughter, Pyrrha, who was prettier than her mother and wiser than her father.

Even my heart softened as I saw her daily fetch water in a jar, pick the grapes, tend the goats.

Even I began to hope for better things from the men and women of Earth, and relented a little from my anger.

A New Beginning

But my hope for better things on Earth did not last long.

I looked down from Mount Olympus and saw the evil things from Pandora's box flying into the hearts of mortal men and women.

I saw fathers beating their sons and wives shouting at their husbands.

I saw children stealing birds' eggs and pulling wings off butterflies.

I saw thieves plundering the mountains for their gold and precious stones, and fighting over them and killing one another.

"The news is bad," said Hermes each time he flew into Olympus. "On all sides the mortals, now they have fire, are growing daily bolder, craftier, crueller..."

So I, Zeus, disguised myself as an ordinary man and, with Hermes, went down to Earth and walked among the mortals to see for myself what use they were making of my fire.

And I saw they were heating metals and forging evil weapons with my fire.

I saw they were burning trees to get more land with my fire.

Worst of all, when I sought hospitality from the fifty sons of King Lycaeon, they gave me a soup made from the bones of one of their very own brothers.

So I sent the flames of my thunderbolt crashing onto their palace, hounded them into the woods and turned them into wolves, so all men go in fear of them and seek to kill them.

And then I cursed Prometheus and Pandora, and my rage was so great that it almost burst the seams of the Universe.

"I will kill them all!" I shouted. "I will wipe them out utterly and for ever!"

I returned to Mount Olympus, and would not listen to Hermes when he begged and begged me to have mercy on his beloved mortals. I strode to the highest crag, raised my arms and thundered:

"A flood! A flood! I will send down a flood. And with this flood I will wash all the evil from the face of the Earth!"

I began to stir the air and darken the sky.

Far below me I saw the mortals scurrying this way and that in panic and fear.

Then, suddenly, I heard the voice of Prometheus, coming from a great distance, but clear enough. He was calling to a young king and his queen as they ran for shelter towards their palace.

Oh, I knew who they were, of course: noble

Deucalion, the son of Prometheus, my arch enemy, and Pyrrha, his sweet wife and daughter of Pandora and Epimetheus. They had given great hospitality to me and Hermes on our travels in disguise.

"Now is the time!" Prometheus was calling to them. "Now is the time to set sail in the ark I told you to get ready. Set sail! Set sail now! For nine days and nine nights you will float upon the waters, and when they go down, you must fall on your knees and beg the great Zeus for mercy. You must beg Zeus for a new beginning!"

The sound of his voice only strengthened my rage.

I raised my arms to the heavens and began to invoke the storm.

"Blow winds!" I ordered. "North, South, East and West! And you, clouds, gather every drop of rain until you are ready to burst like old wine-skins! And you, rivers, swell until your banks burst! And you, all seven seas, turn tempestuous and toss your mighty waves until they dash against the very sky!"

The winds and the waters obeyed my voice, and flooded the Earth for nine days and nine nights.

For nine days and nine nights I watched the waters washing the Earth clean.

For nine days and nine nights I watched that puny little ark carrying Deucalion and Pyrrha upon the vast flood waters.

I could have sent a tidal wave, of course.
I could have drowned the pair of them.
But suddenly I was tired.
Tired of my own anger.
Tired of trickery and treachery.
I longed for peace
To enjoy myself
To feast on nectar and ambrosia
Sit back and listen to Apollo's lyre
To call in the clowns to make me laugh
once more.

Slowly, slowly I let the winds drop and the tempest
die away.

And when dry land appeared again, Deucalion
and Pyrrha did fall to their knees.

"Have pity on us, oh great Zeus," they begged.

"Do not destroy us!"

And Pyrrha held up the box, Pandora's box, my
cruel wedding gift.

"Hope is still here," she cried to me. "Hope is
still with us."

"Oh great Zeus," begged Deucalion, "tell us
how to begin again!"

And I, Zeus, the all-bright, the merciful,
protector of the helpless, took pity on the young
man and his wife.

But I answered them with a riddle.

"You must throw behind you the bones of your mother," I said.

And that brave girl, Pyrrha, called up to me, "No, Zeus! I will do no such thing! Not even for you!"

But Deucalion said, "He means the bones of our great mother, Earth herself! And her bones are these stones!"

And they began to pick up the stones, small and large, scattered upon the ground, and to throw them over their shoulders.

Where Pyrrha's stones fell, they turned into women.

And where Deucalion's stones fell, they turned into men.

And now, here I stand.

I, Zeus,

watching these new mortals mending the Earth I almost destroyed, watching a new world taking shape.

My work is not over.

I must get ready once again to steer the ways of mortals as I steer my chariot across the sky.

My brothers Hades and Poseidon are at my side, my sisters Demeter and Hestia . . .

Hera, my wife . . .

My children, too: Hephaestus, little Hebe and

the hero Herakles

Aphrodite, Artemis and my wise Athene . . .

Hermes the trickster, Apollo and the wine-blooded Dionysus . . .

All of us have work to do to watch over the worlds while

Destiny, Death and Dreams,

Laughter, Luck and the Rainbow

and those three old women at the crossroads carry out their ancient, powerful, mysterious work, joined now by . . . Hope.

Apollo knows what will happen tomorrow and the day after and next year and the year after that.

Apollo tells me the day will come when I will send Herakles to kill the eagle that is pecking at the liver of my great enemy, Prometheus.

He tells me I will forgive him.

He also tells me that Pyrrha and Deucalion will have many fine children who will give birth to new brave mortals . . . even to heroes.

He has even told me their names . . .

Jason

Odysseus

Theseus

Agamemnon and Achilles . . .

Heroic mortals? I cannot wait to see what kind of adventures they will have!

No time to lose!
　　The sun must rise and set again
　　The moon must pull the tides in and out
　　The volcanoes must roar again
　　The rivers flow
　　Spring, summer, autumn and winter
must come and go again and the seas must
carry ships safely to harbour again.

Pegasus is waiting with my chariot.

I crack my whip!

I call up the jagged lightning

And set the sky, the earth and the seas rolling again!

And out of my mighty thunder . . .

I, ZEUS, give the great command to gods, goddesses and mortals:

Begin again!

Let's all begin again!

Characters in the Stories

Gods and other immortals

(The Roman names of the gods and goddesses are
in brackets)

Aphrodite *(Venus)*
Goddess of love; daughter of Zeus and the sea
goddess, Dione, she married Hephaestus.

Apollo *(Phoebus)*
The sun god, music-maker and poet, who each day
rides his golden chariot across the sky; son of Zeus.

Artemis *(Diana)*
Huntress and solitary goddess of the moon; daughter
of Zeus.

Athene *(Minerva)*
Goddess of wisdom, she leapt fully grown from the
head of her father, Zeus.

Demeter *(Ceres)*
Goddess of fruitfulness and the harvest; sister of
Zeus.

Dionysus *(Bacchus)*
Dancing, singing god of wine; the wild, mysterious
son of Zeus.

Hades *(Pluto)*
God of the dark Underworld; brother of Zeus.

Hebe *(Juventas)*
Gentle daughter of Zeus and Hera, her name
means 'youth'; cup-bearer to the gods and
goddesses, she later married Herakles.

Hephaestus *(Vulcan)*
The master blacksmith of the gods; the lame and ugly son of Hera and Zeus.

Hera *(Juno)*
Wife of Zeus; goddess of marriage and motherhood.

Herakles *(Hercules)*
The mighty hero who had to complete his twelve labours without the help of his father, Zeus, who nevertheless, later rewarded him with immortality.

Hermes *(Mercury)*
Mischief-maker and winged messenger of the gods, who moves between Earth and Olympus like a breath of wind; son of Zeus.

Hestia *(Vesta)*
Goddess of hearth and home; sister of Zeus.

Pan
Powerful shepherd-god, half goat, half man, famous for his reed pipes and his sudden loud shout which caused 'panic'. . .

Pegasus
The winged horse, said to be a son of Poseidon born from the neck of Medusa.

Persephone *(Proserpina)*
Beloved daughter of Demeter, and unwilling wife of Hades.

Poseidon *(Neptune)*
God of the oceans; brother of Zeus.

Silenus
Wise old satyr and great friend of Dionysus.

Thetis
The sea goddess who took care of Hephaestus after Hera threw him off Mount Olympus; it was at her wedding that Strife produced the golden apple.

ZEUS *(JUPITER)*
The greatest god of all, ruler of Olympus.

Heroes and mortals

Actaeon
Son of King Aristaeus, a hunter and bee-keeper who was a mortal son of Apollo.

Bellerophon
A prince, whose pride led him to a mighty fall (and who may have been a son of Poseidon).

Deucalion
Son of Prometheus; husband of Pyrrha.

Herakles
See *Gods and other immortals.*

King Midas
A foolish mortal, who learned some hard lessons from the gods.

Pandora
The beautiful but foolish wife of Epimetheus.

Paris
Son of King Priam of Troy.

Perseus
Son of Zeus and a mortal princess, Danae, he became King of Mycenae.

Pyrrha
Daughter of Pandora and Epimetheus; wife of
Deucalion.

Titans

Atlas
The Titan who had to carry the world on his
shoulders.

Cronus
Father of Zeus.

Epimetheus
Brother of Prometheus, husband of Pandora.

Prometheus
Chief of the Titans, bringer of fire to the people on
Earth.

Rhea
Mother of Zeus.